C000126542

Be
More
Tree

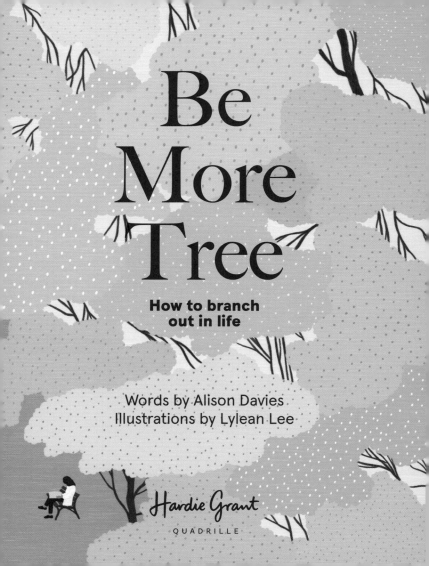

Be More Tree

How to branch out in life

Words by Alison Davies
Illustrations by Lylean Lee

Hardie Grant

QUADRILLE

'Keep a green tree in your heart and perhaps a singing bird will come.'

CHINESE PROVERB

Contents

Imagine: you've been here upon the earth since the dawn of time, a quiet presence, magnificent and majestic. You stand, you breathe, you bear witness. There can be no end to the things you've seen and the lessons learnt. In all this time, you've silently worked your magic, sustaining life, giving freely, blending in with the ebb and flow of the landscape. Without a doubt, this is a feat of extraordinary proportions, a supernatural wonder to match any modern-day mystic or fantasy icon. But then, the humble tree is the mightiest of gurus. No fanfare needed. No fancy accolades to sell this superstar. The tree does what it does, every minute, every hour, every day. It may go unnoticed, unappreciated, even, but the work does not stop. There is no end to the awesomeness of Tree.

Even more amazing, you don't have to do anything spectacular to win favour or experience the magic. It's there on your doorstep. Tree invites you to take a step closer. Stroll deep into the heart of a woody glade. Gaze up at the network of branches. Feel the whisper of bark against hungry palm and let the 'truth of the trunk' imbue you with Zen. The ancients had it sussed. They spoke the language of the trees, believing that each one held a secret, an energy that could be tapped. And while some delivered more obvious gifts, from acorns to fruit and hardy pliable wood ripe for the carving, others were more subtle in their offerings.

You don't have to be a tree-hugger to be more tree (although those in the know recognize there's unlimited joy in a hearty squeeze). You don't have to be one of the many creatures that take refuge in its branches. There's no mystical key or incantation that will unlock the power of this sentient being. The only thing you need to do is bow to the beautiful bough. Celebrate each brilliant branch and bask in the tremendousness that is tree. There, in that moment, *you will find your roots*.

Love
'conkers' all!

Mother Nature is a smart lady. She put the trees in charge. Think 'army of leaf-clothed guardians', and you'll get the merest sapling of a sense of what protection means. When the powers that be made the earth, trees must surely have been their finest work, for theirs is an ethos of care and share. Love unlimited from the ground up. Bound in each branch is an underlying urge to sustain and nurture, stretching to the very tips of the leaves, who for their part, act like supercharged lungs drawing in pollutants and coughing up clean air. An average tree takes in a tonne of carbon dioxide in its lifetime. It also produces around 120kg (260lb) of oxygen. When this tree joins together with his kin, a group of seven or more provide enough of the good stuff to last one human a year; a cluster feeds a family, a forest feeds a town.

These wonders of the wood are the caped crusaders of our time, with a range of climate-busting weapons at their twiggy fingertips. A leafy canopy is the perfect storm shield, allowing water to gently drip and ultimately evaporate before it hits the ground. Their roots are their superhero boots, anchoring them deep in the soil and reducing erosion, while the substantial bulk of the trunk screens noise pollution. Never ones to shy away from a fight, the timbre of their timber means they'll withstand and influence the fiercest wind speeds, reducing temperature and humidity at the same time. Not X-Men, but T-Men; it's all about togetherness. They nurture by nature and while other angst-ridden heroes might suffer at the hands of their demons, trees stand tall in the knowledge that love really does 'conker' all!

Gentle giants, they provide shelter and food for creatures great and small. There's refuge in the open arms of their knobbly limbs, a chance for the tiniest of wing to catch its breath. Furtive furries seeking solace from the biting wind will find safe haven and a bed for the night. Whatever shape or form you take, there's always a nook or cranny to fit, and even a meal for most. Let's not forget that once upon a time humankind made trees their home and used them as a source of nourishment and warmth. Ever hospitable, our leafy hosts keep an open-branch policy and in doing so make a valuable contribution to the ecosystem. This surely makes them the ultimate good Samaritan; not just brawn and brains but a beautiful heart that beats beneath the bark.

Sycamore

Scientific name *Acer pseudoplatanus*

Family *Sapindaceae*

Where to grow Native to central, southern and eastern Europe and western Asia, the Sycamore is widespread, mostly because the seed is extremely fertile. Preferring moist, well-drained soil, this tree loves a sunny spot to thrive. Planted in gardens and parks, it's also a favourite along coastlines because it acts as a wind break.

Appearance The elder of the wood, Sycamore trees can live up to 400 years and grow to a height of 35m (115ft). Pink-grey bark is smooth in young saplings, but cracks with age. The leaves have five lobes and measure between 7 and 16cm (2¾–6½in). The distinctive papery winged fruits, often called keys, are known as samaras.

Fact and folklore The wood from this tree is a popular choice for carving, being pale, strong and with a fine grain. In parts of Wales it is used to make 'love spoons'; more than just kitchenware, these delicately carved spoons are a personal declaration of love and are traditionally given to your sweetheart on St Valentine's Day and to mark special occasions.

Dig deep and find your balance like a tree. These woody sentinels take resilience to the next level and you can do the same with this simple exercise.

Step One
If possible, find a spot outside where you won't be disturbed. This could be in your garden or local park.

Step Two
Stand barefoot on the grass. Feel the cool sensation of each blade as it brushes against your skin.

Step Three
Breathe deeply, roll your shoulders back and lengthen your spine.

Step Four
Turn your attention to the soles of each foot. Notice how they sink into the grass and how the earth supports you.

Step Five

Imagine tiny roots bursting from each sole and stretching deep beneath the surface of the soil. Feel them stretching in every direction, anchoring you to the earth.

Step Six

As you inhale, imagine drawing strength up through those roots and into your body. Feel this energy fill and expand your chest.

Step Seven

Continue to breathe deeply and enjoy the sensation of being fully supported and grounded. It doesn't matter what life throws at you, or how hard those storms hit, you are anchored to the earth.

When life gets tough and you feel vulnerable, bring to mind your tree stance. Whether you're at the office, mid-commute or on a night out, just breathe deeply and visualize roots growing from each foot. Picture them holding you in place as you go about your business. You should feel instantly more secure and confident.

Get twiggy with it

You might not be able to face off a storm, change wind speed or filter the air, but that doesn't mean you're powerless in the face of adversity. Count your blessings and your twigs, and you'll soon be top of the tree!

What to do
Go for a walk in nature and collect a bundle of nicely shaped twigs along the way. Choose ones that are roughly the same size and length, then when you get home tie them together with a ribbon. Each twig represents a quality or skill that you have that can help you. Every day, remove a twig and think of the quality it represents, for example 'your positive attitude' or 'your caring nature'. Say out loud 'this twig represents my caring nature'. Keep them in a decorative bundle and think of one of your many amazing talents for each twig!

Nothing else matters in that moment – it is just you and the trees. There is no past and no future, only the here and now. Standing shoulder to shoulder with the trees is one of the best ways to reduce stress, but if you don't have access to woodland you can re-create this feeling in your own home.

What to do
Take five minutes every day and stand on the spot. Close your eyes and imagine you're in a beautiful wood. The towering trees shield you from the world and you can hear the sounds of nature, the rustle of the leaves, the mellow creak as branches sway into the wind. The deep echoes of an ancient forest call to you. As you breathe in, you smell fern and leaf, dewy grass, the earthy aromas of this magical place. Enjoy feeding your senses in this way. Relax and let the wood draw you in for as long as you want. When you're ready, open your eyes and continue with your day. Remember that at any time, should you feel the need, you can return to this space in your mind.

Silver Birch

Scientific name *Betula pendula*

Family *Betulaceae*

Where it grows Able to thrive in a variety of temperatures, the Silver Birch is widespread throughout the world and can even be found as far north as Lapland. It loves dry woodland and heath, but it's also a popular garden tree.

Appearance Spectral in shade, the Birch is a stunning tree known for its all-year-round silvery white bark and cascade of drooping branches. As the tree matures, the bark sheds wafer thin layers, and over time develops dark diamond-shaped fissures. This striking tree can grow to a height of 30m (98ft) and has small triangular-shaped leaves.

Fact and folklore A symbol of purity and renewal around the world, the Silver Birch was popular with the Celts, who used bundles of birch twigs in a broom or besom to cleanse a space and drive out spirits. Associated with the Celtic goddess Brigid, it was also used in love and fertility rituals. Boughs were often hung over the front door to invite good fortune inside.

Make sharing and caring your ethos.

Consider your network of friends, family and acquaintances. Imagine you're all interconnected branches upon a tree; you all draw strength from each other because you're a part of the whole. To help, sketch a giant tree on a piece of paper and write the names of your nearest and dearest, friends, colleagues and neighbours along each branch. Next, consider ways you can make their lives better. How can you support them and show you care? Write a suggestion by each name, then make a point of implementing a different one each week.

Create a safe haven for the creatures that grace your space. Whether you share your life (including home and garden) with pets, humans or wildlife, make it a woody sanctuary for all!

- Bring the outside in. Fill your home with nature's gifts, from beautiful flowers and pet-friendly plants, to pretty stones, wooden ornaments, carvings and decorative goodies such as pine cones, acorns and conkers.

- Consider your pets. If they're nervous, always make sure they have a safe place to retreat to, should unexpected visitors arrive.

- Position treasured photos of your nearest and dearest around the home. Also include pictures of favourite places and photos from holidays and memorable moments.

- Get green fingered. You might not have room for trees in your garden, but you can fill planters with seeds and bulbs or grow your own fruit and vegetables.

- If you are lucky enough to have a tree, look after it. Trim and care for it, and most importantly spend time beneath its branches.

- Dedicate a patch of your garden to wildflowers. Simply scatter a mixture of seeds and leave them to grow how they would in the wild. Your local friendly bees and butterflies will thank you!

- Make space under hedgerows and fences for hedgehogs and other small mammals to crawl through.

- Get bug friendly and create a bug hotel using old wooden pallets, tiles, moss, dried leaves and any unused terracotta plant pots.

- Put up bird and bee boxes.

- Strategically place bird feeders around your garden. Make sure you put them at the right height so pets can't torment any of your feathered visitors.

- Spread the word – conservation is contagious! Communicate this message to others and show them how they can make a difference.

Channel Dr Dolittle and talk to the animals! Creatures large and small pick up on the personal energy we resonate. They can sense when we're happy or sad. That affects how they respond to us, so get super-friendly and imagine you're greeting an old pal. Send a message of love from your heart to theirs. Put them at ease, just as a graceful tree might open its branches to a new arrival!

Branch out

Branch out

Trees stick together, like glue. They go out on a limb for their kith and kin. While we might stop short, with a nod or a friendly 'hello' to our neighbours, community is key to these savvy sentinels. A quick gossip might satisfy our need for companionship, but trees take communication to the next level, using chemicals, hormones and electrical signals to get their message across. They even have their own Neighbour Wood Watch, not only warning each other when an insect attack is imminent, but also protecting those closest by emitting chemicals that harm those insects. Tree work makes the dream work, and these team players call for back-up by sending airborne signals that attract predators who feed on their assailants. Woodland warfare at its finest!

A tree's sophisticated networking skills are like their roots that spread far and wide, and they make lifelong friends by keeping their interactions alive. Forget Facebook or Twitter; a massive and complex underground network of soil fungi keeps them intrinsically connected. This Wood Wide Web helps them share status updates and nutrients, while also giving them the lowdown on environmental change. Reaching out to each other in this way, means they're constantly in the loop and able to offer support, should a crisis befall them. They know when other trees are struggling and can keep tabs on their nearest and dearest, even administering valuable nutrients to those in the final stages of life.

As long as it's good in the wood, these guys are happy, and that means forming surprising alliances. Fungi might not seem ideal partners in crime to us, but they're an essential part of the family tree. It's all about the trade-off. While fungi cannot photosynthesize, they scavenge among the soil, picking up water and nutrients that they gladly bring back to the tree in exchange for a sugary substance that the tree makes during photosynthesis. This skill swap has worked for thousands of years and could rival any cultural coalition. So while a walk in the forest might seem a sedate affair, there's an unseen world of weaving and intricate dealing taking place, but it's all for the universal good. There's no one-upmanship here. A single sapling never stands alone, for even in the darkest times, when the woodland is under threat, these deeper bonds stay strong. One brain, one heart, a forest united.

Beech

Scientific name *Fagus sylvatica*

Family *Fagaceae*

Where it grows Found throughout Europe, the Common Beech needs humid temperatures and well-drained soil to thrive. Chalk, limestone and light loam soils work best, and once established Beech trees form dense and shady patches of woodland.

Appearance Unlike many other trees, the Beech often holds onto its leaves during the winter months. Massive in height, they can grow up to 40m (130ft), and have a domed crown of foliage. Leaves are oval with a pointy tip. Light green and hairy when young, they turn much darker and lose their hair as they mature. Woody beech nuts are a vital food source for mice, voles and other woodland creatures.

Fact and folklore Mystical Beech is the mother of all trees and called the 'Queen of the Woods' throughout Europe. Its forked twigs are often used as divining rods, while its leaves can be boiled into a healing poultice to relieve swelling. Governed by the Celtic god Fagus, the Beech is associated with wisdom and the first book was thought to have been made from its bark.

Find your forest

Every action has a reaction. Every thought, word and deed, an impact. We are all connected, just like trees in a wood. You might not be able to see the links, but they are there. Subtle psychic threads form every time you meet someone new. These may get stronger, depending on the importance of the relationship. Cement these bonds and improve communication with this simple technique.

Step One
Close your eyes and picture the person you wish to communicate with in your mind.

Step Two
Imagine a cord of light extending from your solar plexus, the area just above your navel. This cord connects you to the other person at the same place.

Step Three
Take a deep breath in and, as you breathe out, visualize a wave of white light travelling from you to the other person, along the cord.

Step Four
See the light hit them in their chest.

Step Five
Take another deep breath, and this time send a message of love along the cord with the wave of light.

Step Six
Picture the person filling up with the warmth of your loving energy.

Step Seven
This technique can also be used if you want to send healing energy to a person. Instead of seeing white light, imagine sending bright blue healing light along the cord.

Try your hand at cosmic ordering, tree style.

Send a powerful message to the universe and state what you'd like to invite into your life. For example, if you'd like a new house, picture it in your mind in as much detail as you can. See yourself walking through the door as the new owner. Freeze frame this image, then picture a network of branches extending from your head, up into the heavens. Imagine sending this image along one of the branches. Say 'It is as I see, by the power of tree!'.

Build branches

Build your network with these top-of-the-tree tips:

- **Reconnect with old friends.** Remember that BFF from childhood, the one you'd climb trees and pretend you could fly with? Root around for their contact details and touch base.

- **Call up your mates.** Switch texting for a phone chat. It might take more time, but you'll benefit from having a real conversation and checking in with each other.

- **When you ask someone how they are,** really mean it. Don't go through the motions, be genuine and show you care how they feel.

- **Start a club.** Whether you're into reading, baking or just hanging out watching movies, get together with your pals and make a regular thing of it. Encourage your friends to bring new friends along and build those connections.

- **Make time for work colleagues.** You might not always get on, but you can improve communications by taking some time out together. Have a coffee and a catch-up at lunchtime or arrange an after-work soirée.

- **Change your attitude.** Don't think of strangers as people you don't know, think of them as friends waiting to happen!

- **Be interested and you'll be interesting.** When meeting people for the first time, show an interest in who they are. Ask open questions to get the conversation flowing and make sure you listen as well as speak!

- **Be kind.** Small acts of kindness go a long way. A smile, a thoughtful word, a polite gesture – they're all saplings which, when given time, will grow and spread further.

Get to know your neighbours.

A cheery hello can work wonders if someone is feeling low. It helps them feel connected. If you know of someone who lives alone, is elderly or vulnerable, offer a helping hand. Little things like getting their shopping for them, weeding the garden or popping around for coffee and cake make a huge difference. The more you get to know your neighbours and your neighbourhood, the more likely you are to notice when someone is really struggling.

Alder

Scientific name *Alnus glutinosa*

Family *Betulaceae*

Where it grows Native to the UK, Ireland and most of Europe, the hardy Alder is a swamp dweller, preferring damp atmospheres and moist ground near rivers, lakes and marshes to grow. Working with the environment, its roots prevent soil erosion. Drier landscapes are also popular with this tree and it can often be seen lining the edges of forests.

Appearance Growing to a height of around 28m (92ft), this tree has dark bark that is often covered with lichen. Twigs are light-brown spotted and also sticky when young. The leaves are dark green and leathery with an indented tip. Male and female catkins appear between February and April.

Fact and folklore Being a swamp dweller, the Alder has a mysterious reputation. When cut, the wood turns a blood orange colour. The ancients, convinced the tree was bleeding, believed it was bad luck to pass one on a journey. The flowers were commonly used to make a green dye, which coloured the clothes of outlaws and was also thought to be the fashion choice of faeries.

Swap shop

When we use money to buy something, we're
making an exchange; one thing for another.
The trees trade with the soil fungi to get exactly
what they want with little effort. The sugary
substance they produce occurs naturally, it's
part of the process and something they do with
ease. You also have a skill set that you can use to
get what you want and make someone else happy.

What to do

- Split a piece of paper into three columns. In the
  first one, make a list of all the things you enjoy
  doing. You don't have to be good at them, these
  are things that make you smile – for example,
  taking the dog for a walk, dancing, and so on.

- In the second column, make a list of all the
  things that you're good at.

- In the final column, make a list of all the things
  you'd like to be good at; these can be things
  that you haven't tried yet.

- To finish, look at the first two columns. Do any of the things you've written link together? Perhaps you enjoy writing poetry and you've been told you're good at giving speeches. You could connect the two by writing themed witty poems for family gatherings and special occasions.

- Now look at your final list. Is there anyone you know who could help you improve or learn any of these skills? Consider if there's a way you can trade skills or learn from each other.

Turn trash into treasure and get into the habit of trading! Have a swap shop party. Invite your mates over, and ask them to bring any unwanted items – anything from clothing to ornaments and books. Have a rummage and see if there's anything you fancy, or you'd like to upcycle. It's a great excuse to re-connect with friends and recycle at the same time!

Be wood wise

Be wood wise

Get up close and personal with a tree and you'll see the etchings of time smothered on the bark. The trunk, which underpins the structure, stands poised; a sombre pillar of truth, with wisdom running like sap through each leafy branch. If trees were human, they'd be scholars with sass. Comfortable in their own leathery skin and rich in mystical insights – the kind of cool we all want to be.

They teach by example, by simply *being* in a world where *doing* is the done thing. Circles of time grace each stump, telling a story of hundreds of years, of thousands of narratives. This is one of the many reasons trees are a symbol of knowledge. There can be no doubt that their longevity gives them power. No wonder humans remain captivated by their charms.

The spiritual significance of trees was not lost on the canny Celts. They believed that each tree had a distinct energy, an aura from which they could draw power and work magical spells and rites. From the sacred Yew, with its drooping branches that formed new trunks where they scathed the ground, a symbol of death and rebirth, to the magical Rowan tree associated with the Celtic goddess Brigid, its wood carved with sigils, and its twigs crafted into wands.

To the Druids, trees harboured mysterious, spiritual beings known as dryads, a term coined by the Ancient Greeks who believed they were female nymphs and guardians of the Oak. Beautiful and ethereal, these spirits lived at the heart of the tree and could roam no further than the coppice in which it stood.

Nordic folk built their entire mythology on one tree. Called Yggdrasil, this giant all-singing, all-dancing Ash held the cosmos together, including the nine worlds. Yggdrasil was the beating heart of all things and should it die the entire universe would crumble. Truly the tree of life, it had a snow-capped crown that reached into the heavens, while a dragon lurked at its base. Lengthy roots stretched into the underworld, and snakes nipped at its trunk. But despite all this, the tree remained a stoic presence, a place for gods and men and a truly epic structure.

Trees lead by example. They live, breathe and give back in verdant swathes of mystic goodness. Sacred knowledge runs from root to tip, from knot to lofty crown. The ancients knew this. They understood their greatness and put them pride of place at the centre of all things. It's time for us to catch up and give these modest mages of the wood the respect they deserve!

Rowan

Scientific name *Sorbus aucuparia*

Family *Rosaceae*

Where it grows Rowan flourishes in the wild, particularly in cooler climates throughout the northern hemisphere. A lover of crags, moors and pine forests, it's also a popular choice for gardens and parks.

Appearance Instantly recognizable for its silvery bark and vibrant scarlet berries, Rowan trees can grow to around 15m (50ft) in height and live for 200 years. Leaves are pinnate and lengthy, comprising of five to eight toothy leaflets. Spring heralds the arrival of clusters of creamy white flowers, and shortly after the bright berry fruit appears.

Fact and folklore Known as the 'witch's tree', Rowan is associated with magic and witchcraft and often used to make ritual wands. The ancients believed it could keep evil at bay and it the trees near houses and graveyards to prevent the dead from rising. The Nordic runes, a collection of symbols that formed the Norse alphabet, were thought to be first carved into the bark of the Rowan tree. It is also associated with rejuvenation and vitality: in Irish myth the Salmon of Knowledge eats the berries of the Rowan tree for longevity.

Fortify your foliage so that you can take on the world, just like Yggdrasil! A strong trunk doesn't need junk of any kind so if you're holding on to baggage, from guilt and fear to bad habits, then it's time to get rid!

Step One
Invest in a fireproof bowl and gather some small twigs, matches, a sheet of paper and a pen.

Step Two
Write down what you'd like to release. If you've a specific worry or fear, set it down on paper.

Step Three
Pop the twigs into the bowl and light with a match. As they burn drop the paper into the flames.

Step Four
Say three times 'Release the junk, strengthen the trunk!'

Sap is crucial to survival. It's the blood that flows through the veins of a tree, a vital substance that delivers mineral nutrients to the furthest reaches. Without it, the tree withers. While we might not run on sap, we do need many forms of sustenance to keep us in tip-top shape, physically and emotionally. Spiritual sap is the stuff of gods. It's the juice that makes the sparkle. Call it soul food; rich, tasty and packed with va-va-voom. Where do you get yours? Answer these questions to find out.

- What brings me peace?

- When do I feel most relaxed?

- How do I de-stress?

- What makes my heart sing?

- When was the last time I was really happy?

- How could I be happier?

- My calm place is ...

- What three changes could I make to my life, to feel more balanced?

Spiritual sap

Get into a mystical mindset and learn more about the power of trees.

Delve into folklore from around the world. Get into all things tree, from stories and pictures of trees, to tree meanings and magic. As you explore, you'll naturally gravitate to a mythology that suits you, or a favourite tree. Take inspiration from this and come up with your own tale, or magical spell. Be creative and have fun. Trees may be sturdy and stoic, but they also dance in the breeze!

Elder

Scientific name *Sambucus nigra*

Family *Adoxaceae*

Where it grows Widespread throughout the world, including Europe and America, Elder is also found in subtropical regions. The Elder is deciduous, growing in woodland, wasteland and scrub.

Appearance With a short trunk and few branches, the Elder is easy to spot if you've the nose for it; its leaves and twigs give off a pungent aroma! It can grow up to 15m (50ft) in height, when fully mature. The leaves are pinnate, and made up of five to seven oval leaflets, while the lemony, white-coloured flowers have five petals.

Fact and folklore Worshipped by the Druids, who believed that it was a gift from the Earth Mother, the Elder is a supremely mystical tree. It was commonly planted near the home to keep the devil at bay and it was thought that if you burnt its wood, you might see the horned one in the flesh! In medieval times, elder twigs were carried for protection, and the dried leaves were tossed into graves to keep the souls of the dead safe as they journeyed to the next life.

Rejuvenate the soul with this mini meditation.

Find a comfortable spot to sit where you won't be disturbed. Close your eyes and focus on your breathing. Inhale to the count of four, and exhale to the count of five. Repeat this action and then start to lengthen each breath by another beat. Visualize a stream of gold light hitting the top of your head, travelling down behind your eyes, into your neck and down the length of your spine. Feel this energizing light splitting off into each limb, reaching your hands, fingers and toes. Continue to breathe deeply as the light floods your entire body. Finally, visualize a cocoon of light around your body, like a giant egg that protects and restores positive energy. Open your eyes, get up slowly and give your body a shake. You should feel energized and upbeat!

Tell it to the trees

Trees are magical. Full of mystical promise. Timeless. They don't judge. They won't interfere, but they can lend an ear and help you find inner peace. When the going gets tough, the tough talk to trees!

What to do

- Get outdoors and find a tree you like. This could be in a local park, the countryside or even your garden. Any tree will do, it's more important that you feel drawn to it in some way.

- Sit beneath its boughs and look up. Take a moment to enjoy the beauty of the tree. Notice how every branch and leaf is connected.

- When you're ready, begin to talk to the tree. You don't have to do this out loud, in your head is fine and works just as well. Tell it your problems, your worries and fears. Tell it your secrets. Whatever you want to get off your chest, tell the tree.

- If it helps, write a list of things you'd like to talk about to keep you on track.

- If you're looking for a solution, ask the tree to send you a sign, to speak to your heart. If you're looking for inspiration, or even a sense of calm, ask the tree to bless you with these qualities.

- Whatever you're looking for, just spending time in the presence of this magnificent being will restore your spirit.

Ash

Scientific name *Fraxinus excelsior*

Family *Oleaceae*

Where it grows Native to Europe, Asia Minor and Africa, the graceful Ash likes fertile, well-drained soil, and prefers to grow together in dense, sloping canopies. A cool environment works best for this tree.

Appearance Tall and slender, Ash trees can reach up to 35m (115ft) in height when fully grown. Easily identifiable in winter for their smooth flattened twigs and velvety black leaf buds, their bark is usually pale brown to grey in colour. The leaves, which lean in the direction of the sun, are arranged in six to eight opposite pairs of oval green leaflets.

Fact and folklore From the same family as the Olive tree, Ash produces an oily substance not unlike olive oil. In ancient times the wood was burnt to ward off evil spirits. Yggdrasil, the Norse world tree, was thought to be an Ash of immense proportions; it was also known as the 'Tree of Life'. The Druids revered this species, using its wood in sacred rites and to make their wands.

Conjure up a little magic with your own tree-inspired wand.

Step one
First, you need to find a nicely shaped twig, something about the length of your arm, from your elbow to wrist. Rowan, Birch and Hazel are all excellent trees to forage, as their wood is highly magical and associated with ancient wisdom. Look around the base of the tree for twigs that have fallen.

Step two
Once you've found something you like, strip off any knobbly or sharp bits that stick out. Smooth the wood down by sanding it, or you can stick with its original form, depending on your preference.

Step three
Decorate your wand with accessories. Crystals and pretty stones can be tied on with ribbon or fixed at the end with wire and glue. Feathers can also be tied around your wand.

Step four

Symbols can be carved into the wood to give it power: for example, a circle represents the cycles of life and the sun; a star is linked to hope and positive energy; and a moon is linked to feminine energy and psychic skills.

Step five

When visualizing what you'd like to attract, hold the wand in both hands and imagine that you're directing energy from your heart through the wand to make your wish come true!

Bend and shape it

Bend and shape it

When the storm hits, the tree bends. Facing off is not an option, for, while the tree might appear rigid in its stance, this clever creeper's greatest strength is its flexibility. Forest Pilates might sound like a fancy new fad, but it's been going on for centuries. The wind blows, the bough bends. It rarely breaks. The breeze is the leader of this woody workout and the tree ebbs and flows to order. And just as Pilates builds a solid core, so the tree builds a sturdy trunk. Scientific research suggests that saplings left weaving in the wind are stronger than those staked to the ground. Change builds resilience in all things. Seasons shift. Leaves fall, like lost lovers cast by the wayside and the tree is left empty, grieving for the summer of its love. But even in its starkness there is no resistance, for to move forward there must be flow.

Greenery grows. Nature is pliable. Whatever the space, the condition, the environment, *it is what it is*. Where there's a wood, there's a way! Take a hint from the malleable Mangrove trees with their stilt-like roots and the ability to filter salt out of seawater. It shouldn't work, but it does. Nothing is impossible to the tenacious tree. While some tree roots extend deep in the ground anchoring them to the earth, others have surprisingly shallow roots – but what they lack in depth, they make up for in length. Trees worry not about what is missing, they work only with what is to hand, like any skilled craftsperson. The twisted branch curves to fit with the undulating landscape, making the tree a contortionist of mammoth proportions. Conclusion: problem solving is child's play for these resourceful plants!

Whether big or small, fat or thin, the tree has learnt to adapt and make the best of every scenario. Trees move with the times, and the weather. While we can dip out of a sudden downpour or avoid gale-force winds entirely, the tree is held captive. But through fixed to the spot, it's still fluid in its approach and able to enjoy the dance of life.

Cedar

Scientific name *Cedrus libani*

Family *Pinaceae*

Where it grows A fan of mountainous climates, Cedar is native to Lebanon and the eastern coast of the Mediterranean and Asia Minor. It's a popular choice for large gardens, estates and parks.

Appearance This evergreen conifer commands attention, growing up to 35m (115ft) in height, with clusters of needles present all year round and several trunks and horizontal layers. This tree is as impressive as it is individual. Barrel-shaped cones, papery to the touch and around 12cm (5in) in length, are produced every other year. Male and female flowers develop as cones, which change colour as they mature.

Fact and folklore The national emblem of Lebanon, the Cedar provides shelter for many species, including the tawny owl, which rests in deep yawning crevices in the bark, and bats, which choose it as a roost. Associated with purification and eternal life, cedar wood is often burned as part of a Jewish tradition to celebrate New Year.

Improve your flexibility and feel the flow with these woody workout tips:

- **Sup for suppleness.** Water is the elixir of life, for trees and humans. Stay hydrated – not only will you feel energized, you'll also improve the elasticity of your skin!

- **Get springy!** Every morning for a couple of minutes do a series of jumps, starting small and then building up to higher, more energetic leaps and star jumps. Imagine you're powered by the wind and, if possible, get outside for this mini workout. A short jumping session every day will get your heart pumping and improve flexibility and movement.

- **Work on your plasticity!** Invest in some playdough and when you're feeling stressed, mould it in your hand. Work your frustrations into the dough and after a couple of minutes swap hands. Not only will you have supple fingers, you'll also be giving the acupressure points on each palm a massage and focusing your mind on something other than your problems.

- **Stretch often.** Introduce regular 'stretch' breaks into your schedule. This is particularly important if you're sat or stood in one position for long periods of time. Work on areas that hold tension, such as shoulders, arms, neck and lower back.

- **Sway.** Stand on the spot and rock from side to side and forward to back. Let your weight shift from heel to toe, and from leg to leg. Get into a rhythm and enjoy this gentle exercise that calms and balances body and mind.

Use garnet to help you navigate a path and adapt to any situation.

It is associated with the root chakra, the body's energy centre situated at the base of the spine. Garnet's deep red colour promotes confidence and flexibility when faced with a challenge; invest in a small piece and keep it with you at all times for strength. Pop it under your pillow before you go to sleep. Trust that your intuition will send you a message via your dreams, and look out for opportunities to take a different, more creative approach.

Trees are nature's problem solvers. They grow where and how they can, making use of the obstacles in their way. Do the same. When a problem hits, take a leaf out of their book and branch out!

Step One

Highlight the issue. This is the trunk of the tree. If it helps, draw a thick column to represent the trunk on a piece of paper and write the problem in the centre.

Step Two

From the base of the column there are roots: these are the root causes of the problem. Consider what these might be – for example, if you're being passed over for promotion at work, this could be because you're not as well qualified as colleagues, you don't have the experience or you feel uncomfortable about putting yourself forward for it. Draw each cause extending from the base of the trunk and write what they are, along each root.

Step Three

Now it's time to branch out. For each root problem, think of an action that you can take to move forwards. For example, if you're not well qualified, perhaps you could take an in-house training course to give you the experience you need. If you're using a diagram, draw on the branches and write the suggestions along each one.

Step Four

Put your plan into action. Pin your diagram somewhere you can see it every day, to help you maintain focus and a positive attitude!

Trees make great counsellors.

They listen. They don't tell you what to do, but they are there for you. Their presence is enough to lift the spirits and help you see the world of opportunities at your fingertips. Next time you're feeling like you've lost your mojo or you're just in need of a pick-me-up, go for a walk in the woods. Instead of focusing on what's bothering you, turn your attention to your surroundings. Take everything in and take your time. Get in flow with nature, and you'll get in flow with life!

Seasonal narratives

Seasons change gradually. It's a transition that the tree takes in its stride, for stride it must, onwards and upwards into each new cycle. There is no avoidance, only acceptance. Life, like nature, moves forwards. Doors close and they open. Chapters end and new ones begin. Your existence is like a story. It has seasons that fluctuate during your lifespan. Where are you in the tale, at this moment?

What to do
Invest in a nice notebook and have a go at journaling your story. You don't have to be a skilled writer to do this. Take a page a day and write something down, for example, how you're feeling right now, an achievement, something you're thankful for, or simply a few words to describe your day. Do this at the same time every day so that you get into the habit, then at the end of a month read back through your entries. You'll notice a pattern or theme emerging, and you'll be able to recognize where you are in your life and where you'd like to go next. Journaling in this way helps identify areas in your life that need work. It will also help you think clearly and restore positive energy.

Check in with yourself every day, with this easy exercise.

Imagine you're a tree in a giant wood. How do you feel? Are you strongly rooted to the spot, connected to the earth and grounded?

Consider your environment. It could be a beautiful spring day, or perhaps there's a nip in the air and your leaves have turned golden.

How do you feel in this moment? Pinpoint the season you're in: spring, summer, autumn or winter.

Make the most of each seasonal phase, by doing things that are appropriate to how you feel. For example, during winter you might be kinder to yourself, allow time for relaxation and eat nourishing food.

During spring, you might put pen to paper and plan some activities, give friends a call and get some dates in the diary or hit the gym.

Hawthorn

Scientific name *Crataegus monogyna*

Family *Rosaceae*

Where it grows Native to the UK, the Hawthorn can be found further afield in North America and Asia. A sun worshipper, this tree flowers best in direct light and is often found growing in hedgerows, woodland and scrub.

Appearance Known for its super-sharp thorny twigs, a mature Hawthorn can grow to a height of 15m (50ft). With dark grey to brown knotty bark, the Hawthorn is also known as the May tree because of the month it blooms. A profusion of creamy white to pink highly scented blossoms smothers the tree, a treat for the eye and nose! Leaves are toothed lobes around 6cm (2½in) in length.

Fact and folklore The Celts believed this tree was the gateway into the fey otherworld, and often inhabited by faeries. Because of this, it was considered bad luck to cut any part of the tree down. One of the first signs of spring, Hawthorn leaves and flowers are often incorporated into May Day garlands. Woodland Hawthorn (*C. laevigata*) has a more pungent aroma, which the ancients likened to the scent of plague victims.

Get your 'grove' on

Get your 'grove' on!

Trees take diversity to the next level. With approximately 60,000 different types around the world, there's no shortage of shapes and sizes to enjoy. Even within the same group, each one is individual. A wooden spear, growing, twisting, curling wherever the fancy takes, formed by circumstance and nature, a one-off. Whatever you're into, you'll find there's a tree for you, and once you find the perfect fit, it will take your breath away. Whether it's a hardy, weather-worn lumbering Oak, or a wafer-thin whisper of a Willow, beauty is in the eye of the beholder, in the connection between human and nature.

Some people admire trees for their elegance, the way they stand and command the catwalk canopy. For others, it's the edgy performers who throw shade that catch the eye, not afraid to wear their curvaceous leaves on the outside and leave a trail of brittle hearts, burnished and tainted by the autumn sun. Then there are those who love the tallest pines: skyscraper thin, these capture the eye and the imagination, going on for what seems forever in a quest to reach the heavens. But for other foliage fans it's not about the way a tree looks, but the job it does and what it gives back to the world that counts. Surface style is superfluous, beneath the bark is where it's at.

A tree's gifts are manifold, from its appearance to other offerings. Think ripe juicy fruit all the colours of the rainbow and a potpourri of pretty spring blossom. Nuts, seeds and berries that tantalize taste buds, perfectly formed pine cones and shiny bright conkers, not to mention the delicate detail of an acorn in its cup. Leaves like spades and those like scissors, razor-sharp fineness, sweet-scented pine-ness; a joy to the senses, all spiny and fresh. The feast of a forest can be quite overwhelming. There's so much to take in and to take for granted, but once you have sat at the table you'll never go back. For, while a lone tree is unique and a thing of beauty, a group clustered together all wild and woody is the artist's finest moment, a masterpiece of Mother Nature.

Trees huddle by design; they form constellations that bring together their strengths, for there is power in numbers. A sense of sanctuary in the thickest of thickets. And it's the same for us. As individuals we are one-of-a-kind exceptional, but when we join forces we bring together the very best bits to create our own fairy-tale wood.

Hazel

Scientific name *Corylus avellana*

Family *Betulaceae*

Where it grows Abundant in most of Europe, parts of north Africa and western Asia, Hazel is found in hedgerows and scrub, and in the understory of woodland.

Appearance When left to grow in nature, Hazel trees can reach a height of 12m (40ft) and usually live for around 80 years, although coppiced trees can lives into their hundreds. Young trees are blessed with smooth, dark brown bark, but over time this cracks and greys. Clusters of catkins, like fluffy lambs' tails, appear in mid-February and are soon followed by the leaves. Rounded and palm-shaped, these form a pointed tip and are soft to the touch because of their downy underside.

Fact and folklore A popular food source for moths, butterflies and dormice, the Hazel also has magical status. In medieval times it was associated with fertility and its nuts were carried as charms to prevent ill health. The hazel was also known as 'The Tree of Knowledge' and eating its fruit could bring instant enlightenment, while its wood was a favourite of witches, who used the rods as wands.

Don't be shy! Believe in yourself. It doesn't matter who you are, what you look like or how you feel; you are awesome. Make like the finest fir in the forest and strike a pose!

Step One
Stand in front of a full-length mirror.

Step Two
Rather than focus on things that you don't like, take in the whole view of yourself. From top to toe, consider how marvellous you are. How your body works for you in so many different ways.

Step Three
Look yourself in the eye and smile. See how it lights up your face. Take this a step further and pose as if you're a supermodel on the catwalk. Throw your shoulders back, tuck your tummy in and tighten your core muscles. Tilt your chin up and throw your best pout.

Step Four
Say 'I am amazing. Every part of me is amazing. I amaze myself!' Repeat several times until you really believe it.

Words are like the leaves that cloak a tree. They build a story, which becomes a picture that we carry around. If the words you use to describe yourself are negative, the narrative that you believe in is also negative and, ultimately, your self-confidence will suffer. Shed the negative words and give yourself space to breathe and grow beautiful new buds of hope and optimism.

What to do
Over the space of a week, write down any negative thoughts that spring to mind on separate pieces of paper. At the end of the week, light a candle and pass each paper through the flame. Drop it into a fireproof bowl to burn to ash. When you've finished say 'I shed these words like leaves. I replace negative with positive and with every breath my beauty blossoms.'

Strut your 'trunky' stuff and get your 'grove' on by dancing up a storm in your living room. Make sure you won't be disturbed. Stick on your favourite dance number and throw some shapes. Go a step further and get all dressed up to do it. It doesn't matter that you're not heading out or that no one will see you. You will look and feel fabulous, and you are all that matters!

Apple

Scientific name *Malus x domestica*

Family *Rosaceae*

Where it grows Found in Asia, Europe and North America, the Apple tree infiltrates hedgerows and thickets, and can also be seen at roadsides and in copses.

Appearance Not a huge climber, the Apple tree usually grows up to 10m (32ft) high, but what it lacks in size it makes up for with glorious blooms and fruit. Bark is scaly, grey and lined with ridges, while the fern-green leaves have serrated edges and a woolly underside. Apple tree blossom is a common sight in May and June: these five-petalled flowers range in hue from white to soft pink. It takes an Apple tree four to five years to produce its first harvest of fruit, which can be green or red, and an array of different flavours, depending on the species.

Fact and folklore A potent symbol in mythologies around the world, the apple takes centre stage: it was the fruit of eternal youth to the Norse gods, and synonymous with temptation in the Christian faith. To the Ancient Greeks, the apple (and the Apple tree) was associated with the goddess of love, Aphrodite. To propose, young men would throw an apple at their chosen sweetheart. If she caught it, the answer was 'yes'.

97

Know your worth by treating yourself at least once a week.

You'll get more out of the experience if you do something that delights the senses, such as buying a pretty bunch of flowers and placing them somewhere you can see them every day, or indulging in a luxurious soak in the bath with candles and scented oils. Make sure you treat a different sense each week, so if your first choice is to cook a delicious meal, your second might be a massage or a facial.

Consider the ways you can work together with other leafy lovelies, whether on a personal or professional level. Joining forces can turn an empty field into a meadow of opportunity!

What to do

- **Walk together.** Whether you are part of a social walking group, or just fancy some company on your journey into work, find a walking buddy or two and use the time to connect and share ideas.

- **Train together.** Assemble a gym gang, from two to ten people; you'll keep each other motivated, have fun, set goals and even celebrate those milestone successes!

- **Play together.** Whatever you enjoy doing in your spare time, from dancing till dawn to sharing a meal, make sure you do it with friends. Why should the kids have all the fun? Put regular play dates into your diary and stick to them.

- **Cry together.** Sometimes you just want to curl up and wallow, but if you're having a tough time emotionally and you need some support, don't be afraid to ask your nearest and dearest. Put the call out, invite your BFFs over and share the woe. You'll benefit from the empathy and getting things off your chest, and you may even get some sage advice.

- **Date together.** Double date, triple date or throw a party, but enjoy dating with friends and their partners, and you'll see a different side to your love interest and vice versa. You'll meet new people, share laughs and build healthy relationships.

- **Meditate together.** Take time out in a group and set up regular meditation sessions to de-stress. Doing this together will ensure you stick with it, rather than putting it last on your list. You'll also build a relaxed camaraderie with your new Zen buddies.

Have a tree-planting party.

On a sunny day, get everyone round and get them involved. Give the occasion some ceremony and say a few words as you're gathered together, then eat, drink and be merry. Even if you don't have ambitions to build a forest in your back garden, a planting session with friends is a great way to catch up and do something good for the environment. You might also get some free gardening out of it!

Ginkgo

Scientific name *Ginkgo Biloba*

Family *Ginkgoaceae*

Where it grows Although it's native to China, the hardy Ginkgo thrives in most temperate and Mediterranean climates. Resistant to pollution and pests, this stalwart of the tree world, is a popular choice and decorates cities around the world.

Appearance Growing up to 40m (130ft) in height, this striking tree has corky, ashen grey bark and fan-like leaves that spread up to 12cm (4¾in) in width and are often deeply notched. The leaves produce two lobes, which is where the tree gets its name from. The Japanese call it 'I-cho', meaning 'leaves like a duck's foot'. Producing both male and female flowers, the fruits develop late autumn.

Fact and folklore Known as the Maidenhair tree in England, the ancient Ginkgo has graced the earth for around 200 million years. With a lifespan of up to 3,000 years, each tree bears many gifts, from its distinctive seeds, which have been used as a food source for centuries, to its leaves, which contain ginkgolides, thought to improve blood circulation and relieve Alzheimer's. The Ginkgo was originally cultivated by Buddhist monks, who wisely chose it as their sacred tree.

Let nature nurture

Anyone who has spent time in the company of trees
will acknowledge the healing effect – the sense of
vitality – that exudes from each coiled branch. As
you drift idly through a dense patch of woodland,
feel the cleansing aura of the trees envelope you
in a warm embrace. There's nothing like it, and
science agrees! Research concludes that being in
the presence of trees is not only good for the soul,
but the body too, lowering the heart rate and blood
pressure, reducing stress and generally improving
mental health. Studies show that the sinuous sight
of a tree accelerates healing, by reducing stress
and pain in the patient and allowing the immune
system to work more effectively. What's not to love?

Trees are nature's medics, dispensing a huge
prescription of calm, as well as to helping us
breathe. They lead by example, cleansing the
space (and themselves) by drinking huge amounts
of water. A large Oak consumes at least 450 litres
(100 gallons) of water a day. There's no skimping
on hydration: it's the basis of survival. Drawing up
ground water from the deepest tap roots, they also
give the soil a helping hand by changing its physical
structure. As they decompose, fallen leaves and
twigs provide organic matter, which seeps into the
soil and allows it to absorb more liquid. Being part
of the water cycle, trees en masse play a vital role

Let nature nurture

and can prevent droughts simply by being there. While the roots are busy guzzling, the leaves are doing their bit too, releasing vapour into the air. This process, known as transpiration, occurs when water, drawn up from the roots, evaporates from the leaves and forms rain clouds. Science has discovered that forests are responsible for almost half of all rainfall, making them game changers in the war against climate change.

While all trees do their bit for wellbeing, some species go even further. The Willow tree is a prime example. Its bark contains the active ingredient salicin, which is used in over-the-counter aspirin. The White Willow, in particular, is thought to have the most potent bark, which can be used in infusions to soothe aches and pains. The Elder produces berries and flowers that have powerful flu-fighting properties, while pine needles are packed with vitamin C, and can be turned into vinegar or tea. Silver Birch, an elegant sweet-scented tree, is an antiseptic powerhouse from leaves to sap, and the inner bark is often used to treat fever.

Trees reveal their secrets slowly, harbouring hidden depths that we can only imagine. Healers at heart. Saviours of the soul. It's time we returned the favour, for in saving the trees, we save ourselves.

White Willow

Scientific name *Salix alba*

Family *Salicaceae*

Where it grows Native to Europe and western and central Asia, the White Willow favours wet ground and can be found growing by rivers, streams and lakes.

Appearance This tree gets its name from the white underside of its slender leaves. The pallor comes from a felty covering of white hairs. The largest species of Willow, mature trees can grow up to 25m (82ft) in height. Twigs are pliable and slim, extending from a grey-brown trunk. The sloping crown appears to lean, giving this tree its striking appearance.

Fact and folklore A symbol of endurance, still flourishing even when bent into extraordinary shapes, the Willow is revered by many cultures. The Native Americans tied willow branches to their boats and homes, believing the tree would protect them from storms. In Europe people used a similar practice to prevent bad luck from entering the home. The Chinese also placed the branches in doorways, to keep evil at bay.

Tree shower

You can absorb the healing power of Tree by simply being in its presence. Try an invigorating tree shower to cleanse mind and spirit.

What to do

Find a tree that you like the look of; choose one that you can easily sit beneath. Position yourself with your back against the trunk and press back into the bark. Imagine that with every outward breath you fall further into the tree. Continue to do this until you feel like you are part of the tree, joined bark to skin. Look up into the network of branches and feel the light filtering between the leaves, showering you with the sun's rays. Close your eyes and turn up the brightness of this light. Finally, picture the leaves coming down in a shower, bathing you in a blanket of green goodness.

Pine needle vinegar makes a tasty alternative to balsamic, and it's also packed with vitamins. Make your own with this easy recipe.

- Start by removing pine needles from the branch of a douglas fir (*Pseudotsuga menziesii*). Holding the branch in one hand, using the other, gently pinch and slide your hand down the stem. This strips off all the needles quickly and easily.

- Take a handful of pine needles and wash them carefully.

- Pop in a clean jar so they are tightly packed, then cover with apple cider vinegar.

- Store in a cold dark place for around six weeks.

- Take a tablespoon a day to boost levels of vitamin C or add to a mug of hot water and honey, as relief for a cold.

BE MORE TREE

Stand silently
among the trees and
you'll feel an aura of
peace, a deep sense
of wellbeing.

Trees do it naturally. They're constantly drinking deep and finding ways to consume more water. You too can give yourself a deep cleanse and increase your fluids with these top tips.

- **Drink a glass of warm water first thing.** You'll be dehydrated from a night's sleep and this will help to wake you up, while being gentle on the digestive system.

- **Sip water throughout the day.** You don't have to glug glass after glass if you don't want to, but sipping a couple of glasses as you go about your business, will increase your hydration and boost energy levels.

- When you feel like having a snack, **drink a glass of water instead**. We often feel hungry when we're dehydrated, so reach for the water first and replenish your system.

- **Eat lots of watery vegetables.** They're an important source of water, and, rather than going straight through you and flushing out nutrients, water from vegetables comes with antioxidants, anti-inflammatory agents and fibre. Water-rich foods include cucumber, tomatoes, spinach, lettuce, broccoli and apples.

- **Go wild, and drink from the source.** The next time you're out and about in the countryside, sip fresh from a spring or mountain waterfall, taking care to follow simple safety guides: drink from a flowing stream (not still water) and ensure the water is clear, not muddied or near livestock.

English Oak

Scientific name *Quercus robur*

Family *Fagaceae*

Where it grows Known as the 'King of the Wood', the English Oak is a common sight in woodland and forests throughout Britain. The second most common tree, after the Birch, the Oak has become the UK's national emblem. Other species such as the Holm (*Q. ilex*) and the Red Oak (*Q. rubra*) grow in Europe and North America.

Appearance Sturdy in trunk, with a vast and spreading canopy, the Oak is a distinctive tree. Growing up to 40m (130ft) in height, it often shortens with age to improve its lifespan. Leaves grow in bunches, up to 10cm (4in) in length and have four to five lobes. Acorns in dainty cupules form on the stems. When ripe and berry brown they fall to the forest floor to sprout the following spring.

Fact and folklore The mighty Oak has been revered since ancient times. The Greeks associated it with their god of thunder, Zeus, likely because the trees were often struck by lightning. The Romans wore crowns of Oak leaves as symbols of their power. To the Druids, the Oak was a magical tree, and they would perform sacred rituals in Oak groves.

Water hydrates the mind, and the soul.

When you're feeling stressed and you need clarity, hold both wrists under the cold tap for a couple of minutes. Let the water flow quickly and breathe deeply. Delight in the icy sensation as the water hits your skin. Focus on nothing else but your breathing and the feel of the water.

Afterwards, you should feel instantly calmer. You will be more mentally alert, and better able to deal with a crisis, too!

Do your bit to save the trees by planting one from seed. You'll need some compost, a plant pot with holes in the base, some stones, wire mesh and the seeds itself: acorns, sweet chestnuts and hazelnuts work well.

Step One
Put a handful of stones at the bottom of the plant pot, then fill to the top with compost.

Step Two
Plant your seeds about 2cm (¾in) down from the top of the compost, and give them plenty of water to help them germinate.

Step Three
Position the pot outside and cover the top with wire mesh to prevent the birds from getting at your seeds. Also, make sure the pot is in a shaded spot.

Step Four

Keep checking the soil for dryness. Water regularly, but don't drown the seeds.

Step Five

When they begin to sprout, transfer the seedlings to a bigger pot to give them room to breathe and grow.

Step Six

When the shoots reach around 40cm (16in) tall, it's time to plant them in the ground. If you have more than one, be sure to leave at least 2m (6½ft) between each plant so the roots can spread.

Step Seven

Keep your saplings protected from the frost and clear of weeds and grass; this allows them full access to all the nutrients they need in those early stages of development.

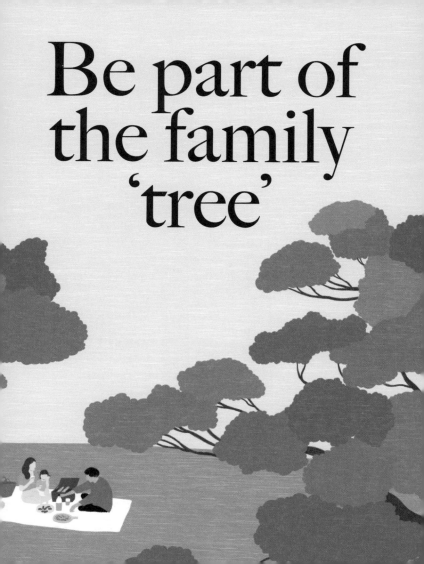

Be part of the family 'tree'

New life is like a tree; a tiny shoot reaching for the stars, finding passage through the soil and taking root on the earth. Growing, stretching, getting stronger. Forming branches and trying each direction for size. Testing the air, going with the ebb and flow of the seasons in a continual cycle of rebirth, making connections, friends, forming unseen bonds. Bearing the storm and the sunshine in equal measure. Wilting and waning. Growing tired and brittle, but still standing with poise and the knowledge of time. Peaceful and at peace within those shards of bark. Then, slowly and with grace, returning to the earth to be met by Mother Nature's soft embrace. A life complete, yet not quite finished. A never-ending circle. The tree of life goes on.

Birth, death and rebirth are a walk in the park for the average tree. It's a fact. They can live for hundreds of years, but they do not shy away from the inevitable. Dead wood takes centre stage, playing its part in the ecosystem. Giving back during decomposition, it provides nitrogen and a number of valuable nutrients, not to mention microhabitats for a range of creatures. Stumps and snags are the perfect comfort stop for those on the wing, a home from home, where furry and feathered friends can rest, eat and take refuge. For a snake on the move, a log is the ideal sun lounger, a place to chillax, soak up the rays and regulate body heat. And should the need arise, a bolt hole from the stresses of the real world. Woodpeckers, true to their name, peck and scavenge for food, and often nest in dead cavities on trees. For, while one part of the trunk may have withered, it is still connected to the land of the living. Just as we have a family tree and a way of connecting us to the past.

All life needs its roots; a web of time that we can trace back to the beyond, to those people and things who helped shape us and our future. Some family trees are vast and complex, like interwoven tubers beneath the earth, while others are sparse, their stems short but strong. The tree is a model for our journey through life. Nature's blueprint for us. Death is not the end, but a powerful transition from one state to the next. The wood may have wilted, but it's part of the tree and always will be. Timeless, enduring, the ultimate guru.

Yew

Scientific name *Taxus baccata*

Family *Taxaceae*

Where it grows Native to western, central and southern Europe, northwest Africa, northern Iran and southwest Asia, Yew trees are often used as hedging plants and form the understory of Beech woodland. They're also commonly found in church graveyards.

Appearance One of the longest-living trees in northern Europe, the Yew is easy to distinguish thanks to its evergreen, needle-like leaves, which are present all year round. These sharp, pointed needles grow either side of the twig. The tree's bark is reddish brown but with a purple tint. Mature Yews can grow to a height of up to 20m (65ft).

Fact and folklore Associated with death and decay, Yew trees were originally planted in churchyards as a way of purifying the dead. As they were highly toxic, this practice also served to stop people from grazing their cattle on hallowed land. The Romans believed that Yew trees were formed in hell, while Yew branches have also been carried at funerals and considered symbols of immortality.

Life is full of ups and downs. We can be riding high at one moment, and back at the bottom of the tree the next. Know when you're waxing and waning and move through each phase with relative ease by taking inspiration from the tree's life cycle.

Step One
Curl up in a small ball on the floor. Imagine that in this state you're a tiny seed about to burst through the soil.

Step Two
Slowly unfurl from the ball shape and rock back on your knees. Sit in this position and lengthen your spine. Breathe and take in your surroundings.

Step Three
Place your palms together in a prayer position, and gradually extend both arms above your head, weaving them as you go, like a tiny sapling twisting and turning as it bursts through the soil.

Step Four
Step by step, get on your feet. Look up at the ceiling and continue to stretch upwards.

Step Five
Open your arms and create a V shape, like a tree extending its branches. Hold this position for the count of ten.

Step Six
Slowly bring your arms down until they're relaxed at your side, lower your head and look at the floor. Breathe deeply and relax.

Step Seven
Weave and curve your body, bringing it down to the floor until you're kneeling again.

Step Eight
Resume your original ball position as you return to the ground to be reborn once more.

Try this mini visualization to help you reach your goals.

Picture yourself standing in front of an enormous pine tree. As you look up, you can see that it stretches so high, you can't spy the top. Take a deep breath and imagine you're climbing the tree with ease. Propelled forward at speed, you're scaling higher and higher. Springing from branch to branch like a monkey, you can feel the breeze against your face. You can see the pinnacle of the tree in sight. You fly faster than ever and with one final leap reach the top. Take a moment and take in the view; see the tips of the trees below you and the clouds that surround you. Say 'I reach the top with ease!'

Celebrate the diversity and meaning of the tree of life, by creating a tree calendar for the next 12 months.

What to do
Assign a tree to each month, for example, you might associate the Ash with January, the Yew with February, and so on. Keep a note of this somewhere prominent. During that particular month learn everything you can about the tree: what it looks like, where it grows, what the leaves look like, any fascinating facts, folklore, symbolism, and so on. Celebrate the tree in some way: anything from spending time with it outdoors, to finding a picture of it and placing it somewhere in your home. By the end of the year you'll have a deeper understanding of trees, and you'll also benefit from spending time in nature.

Play this game with a friend. Ask each other the following question:

'If you were a tree, what type of tree would you be and why?'
Set a time limit of five minutes and both write down your immediate thoughts.

Next, ask each other this question:

'If I were a tree, what type of tree would you choose for me and why?'
Again set a time limit of a couple of minutes and write down your thoughts. Then share what you've written with each other. You'll get an insight into how you feel about yourself and also how others see you.

Holly

Scientific name *Ilex aquifolium*

Family *Aquifoliaceae*

Where it grows Found across Europe, Asia and north Africa, Holly thrives in Oak and Beech woodland, hedgerows and scrub.

Appearance This prickly tree is best known for its inky green leaves with their high shine and the bright red berries that adorn its branches throughout the winter. Growing up to 15m (50ft) in height, Holly has the potential to live for around 300 years. Its bark is dark brown and smooth, but often covered in warts.

Fact and folklore A favourite of the mistle thrush, who guards the berries during winter to prevent other birds from stealing them, this tree is steeped in folklore as a symbol of fertility and eternal life. For centuries, Holly has been used to decorate homes during the festive season. Druids, however, believed that cutting down the branches would bring bad luck. The leaves and berries from the plant are thought to ward off witches and the devil.

Trace your tree

Get to the root of who you are, and reconnect with your family, past and present, with these tops tips.

- **Get talking.** One of the best ways to find out more about your ancestry and to get a sense of who you are is to ask questions. Have those conversations with relatives. Start by sharing memories and ask them what it was like when they were young and what they can remember about their parents/grandparents. Give them a focal point, for example: 'Gran, what was school like when you were a child?' As they begin to describe their past, other things will emerge and you'll have the opportunity to ask questions about their life, the things and people they knew, and so on.

- If you want to **go down the official 'root'**, get together a selection of names and dates of your relatives and request birth and death certificates and census details to help you piece together their lives, then write this up in a form that's easy for you to understand.

- **Get under the skin.** If there's an ancestor you feel particularly drawn to, find out as much as you can about them and their life, then have a go at writing their story. Use your imagination and tell it in their voice. This will help you connect with them on a deeper level. If writing isn't your thing, get creative in another way, for example, by drawing a picture of what you think they might have looked like.

- **Hold a remembrance ceremony** and honour your ancestors. If you have old photographs, lay them out where you can see them. Light a candle, and give thanks for your forebears, for the path they laid for you. Say a few words out loud or in your head, and spend some time reflecting on your own life and where you're at right now.

If you've been rooting around in the past, you might have discovered familiar likenesses and traits that recur throughout your tree. Are there any special talents that your family have passed down to you? If so, celebrate them in some way. Give thanks for the unique gifts that you've inherited. Repeat this affirmation every day, 'I am grateful for the gifts of my ancestors. I am held strong by my roots.'

Publishing Director Sarah Lavelle
Senior Commissioning Editor Harriet Butt
Senior Designer Emily Lapworth
Illustrator Lylean Lee
Head of Production Stephen Lang
Production Controller Sinead Hering

Published in 2021 by Quadrille, an imprint
of Hardie Grant Publishing

Quadrille
52–54 Southwark Street
London SE1 1UN
quadrille.com

All rights reserved. No part of this publication may be
reproduced, stored in a retrieval system or transmitted in
any form by any means, electronic, mechanical, photocopying,
recording or otherwise, without the prior written permission
of the publishers and copyright holders. The moral rights of
the author have been asserted.

Cataloguing in Publication Data: a catalogue record for this
book is available from the British Library.

Text © Alison Davies 2021
Illustrations © Lylean Lee 2021
Design and layout © Quadrille 2021

ISBN 978 1 78713 6243

Printed in China